BILLY GRAHAM

Evangelistic Associatio

Always Good News.

D0204833

Dear Friend,

I am pleased to send you this copy of *A Peace of My Mind* by Stuart Briscoe. Stuart has authored more than 40 books and has taught at the Billy Graham Training Center at The Cove.

In this book, Stuart explores the mystery of finding perfect peace in God. He challenges believers to redirect our focus from the chaos, conflicts, and stresses of our circumstances to the orderliness of God, who "*will keep him in perfect peace, whose mind is stayed on You*" (Isaiah 26:3, NKJV). I pray that God will bless you with the peace that passes all understanding as you seek Him.

For more than 60 years, the Billy Graham Evangelistic Association has worked to take the Good News of Jesus Christ throughout the world by every effective means available, and I'm excited about what God will do in the years ahead.

We would appreciate knowing how our ministry has touched your life. May God richly bless you.

Sincerely,

Franklin Graham
President

If you would like to know more about our ministry, please contact us:

IN THE U.S.:
Billy Graham Evangelistic Association
1 Billy Graham Parkway
Charlotte, NC 28201-0001
BillyGraham.org
info@bgea.org
Toll-free: 1-877-247-2426

IN CANADA:
Billy Graham Evangelistic
 Association of Canada
20 Hopewell Way NE
Calgary, AB T3J 5H5
BillyGraham.ca
Toll-free: 1-888-393-0003

a peace of my mind

Stuart Briscoe

This *Billy Graham Library Selection* is published with permission from Life^n Books, LLC.

A PEACE OF MY MIND
By D. Stuart Briscoe
Published by LIFEⁿ BOOKS, LLC
in partnership with Dunham+Company

www.peaceofmymind.org

Neither D. Stuart Briscoe nor LIFEⁿ BOOKS, LLC or Dunham Books is engaged in giving any professional counseling, psychotherapeutic, legal, accounting, or investing services. If professional advice is needed, please seek out the proper professional. We disclaim any loss, either directly or indirectly, as a consequence of applying the information presented herein.
First published in the United States of America by LIFEⁿ BOOKS, LLC
©October 2010 by D. Stuart Briscoe
All rights reserved.

THE LIBRARY OF CONGRESS HAS CATALOGED THIS EDITION OF THE BOOK AS FOLLOWS:
Briscoe, D. Stuart
A PEACE OF MY MIND

ISBN: 978-1-59328-401-5
Previous ISBN: 978-1-937033-06-4
Library of Congress Control Number: 2010906486

Discipleship—Christianity;   Education—Christian

Cover Design by: Hope Certalic
Cover Photo: iStockphoto

To my partners in ministry at

TELLING THE TRUTH

Dear brothers and sisters in the Lord

committed to sharing the abundant life in Christ

with people all around the world!

Contents

PUBLISHER'S PREFACE

It has been said often, of late, that "the future is not what it used to be." This is a funny line, but what people mean by it is actually quite serious.

What we mean is that the times – *our times* – are out of sorts, that things are not as good as they should be. Nostalgia warms and brightens the past, and we feel as if our lot is tougher than the lot of others who have journeyed before us, in bygone days.

Every age will have its share of troubles. This classic book by Stuart Briscoe on the peace of God is set in an England under Hitler's siege. That is trouble enough.

But it is, ironically, in the very depths of trouble that we draw from the well of peace. Some of us have been there, but the well we have drawn from offered nothing. Others of us have drawn from a well that has refreshed us. We have learned that *we cannot refresh ourselves* in times when peace eludes us.

And that is the key to this amazing story, written by an amazing man. Meandering masterfully through the grand biblical narrative as well as through his own remarkable life, through momentous history and through common stories – and then connecting all of these things to our own stories – Dr. Briscoe explains how peace, *perfect peace*, can be ours.

And that there is only one way to get it.

At a time when so many thirsty people are digging wells in all the wrong places, this faithful ambassador for God offers an important message for all of us. Given the association between the Briscoes and their ministry, Telling the Truth, and the Billy Graham Evangelistic Association over the span of many decades, we are especially excited about this book project.

Enjoy the journey!

Jim Van Eerden
Life^n MEDIA
Magnalia Forest, North Carolina

chapter 1

The Longing for Peace

In 1930 I was born in Millom, Cumberland, in the extreme northwest corner of England. To the west the Irish Sea lapped or roared, depending on the vagaries of the weather, on endless sandy beaches. To the east and south the Duddon river flowed quietly into a wide estuary where over the years unwary fishermen and travelers had been trapped in quicksands. To the north a low range of hills seasonally green, brown, or purple were home to flocks of hardy sheep.

But beautiful as the surroundings were, the real secret to Millom lay far beneath the surface. The town existed because someone had discovered under the idyllic countryside one of the world's richest seams of iron ore. Iron was the life blood of the town. The mines and the smelting "iron works," as we called them, provided the livelihoods for many of the people among whom I grew up. As long as the seam kept producing, life in Millom survived.

The down side of the iron industry was the ugly grey "slag banks" comprised of the dross left over from the smelting process that dominated the town. Year after year, they grew longer and higher and the south end of the town lived perpetually in their shadows. Day and night trains of buggies climbed the slag banks like dusty caterpillars and poured their loads of molten slag in golden rivers down the grey sides of the man-made mountains. Then, for a few brilliant moments, the town glowed until the slag cooled and the dull routine of day or night resumed.

A couple of times someone miscalculated. On one occasion the driver of the train was not made aware of the bombing alert, and on pouring out the molten dross during a World War II nighttime bombing raid, he inadvertently lit up the town. Luftwaffe crews flying their bombers high overhead accepted the gift with relish and pounded the inviting and illuminated target of my home town with high explosives. Kids my age perished, and I tried to process their sudden brutal passing as I stood mutely before what was left of their houses the next morning.

Millom itself in no way threatened the designs of Hitler. But Barrow-in-Furness, a mere dozen miles away as the crow or bomber flies, did. For it was there that Vickers-Armstrong built ships for the Royal Navy. Sleek, black submarines and great grey aircraft carriers rejoicing in such names as *Illustrious*, *Indomitable*, and *Indefatigable* were launched, fitted out, and passed their trials, before taking on their crews and sailing off to battle. When German intelligence became aware that these ships were near completion, we braced for nightly air raids. The midnight wailing sirens, the earth-shaking thumps of detonations and vibrations producing endlessly rattling windows, and the constant dinning of the Westminster chimes of the clock on the dining room wall made impressions vividly remembered to this day.

How did German intelligence gather its material? It was presumably through spies on the ground who were well prepared. For during the sad, dark days prior to the War when it became obvious that Europe was once more sliding towards the abyss, the Luftwaffe sent a giant airship over my home town en route to Barrow-in-Furness to spy out the land and photograph the shipyards. The sight of that huge and ominously silent craft displaying the great black Iron Cross hovering over my home and my school – my town – is one of the most indelible recollections of my childhood. More than sixty years later I can still recall the looks of anxiety on the faces of our neighbors as we rushed into the streets not knowing what we were looking at, but knowing that we did not like it!

At that moment I knew fear – for how else can a small boy react when he sees something in the sky menacing and silent and gliding inexorably about its business of intruding in his life? *And how could he forget it?* I had been introduced to the fear-inducing uncertainties of life, and for the next six years – critically formative years – I experienced the absence of peace and the presence of war.

But as the weary years of war dragged on, we adjusted. Food rationing no doubt presented my mother with all kinds of culinary problems, but we managed. Word came that many of the men from Millom who served in the Border Regiment had been captured in Singapore and were languishing in Japanese prisoner-of-war camps, but we hoped they were alright.

But over our heads and in our hearts loomed the constant specter of the Invasion. We all believed it was only a matter of time until the Germans would arrive on our shores or land in our fields. We listened to Winston Churchill on the radio promising us nothing but "blood, sweat, and tears" and we knew he had warned Hitler that if he invaded our shores, "we shall defend our island, we shall fight on the landing grounds, we shall fight in the fields and in the streets, we shall fight in the hills; we shall never surrender." The thought of all this fighting talk stirred our British blood but did nothing to hide the pervasive sense of apprehension that one night the bells of St. George's Church would ring out the message that the Nazis had arrived; that we had to do what Churchill had said. We lived with a gnawing sense of discomfort – *of disease.*

I remember the first time the sirens wailed in the middle of the night. We all rushed down to a corner of the cellar which served as a warehouse for my father's grocery store. This was the nearest thing to an air raid shelter available, and I have no recollection of feeling sheltered or secure. I was only cold and scared. There we sat and looked at each other waiting for we knew not what. Silently we huddled in our nightclothes surrounded by sacks of flour and the incongruously pleasant smell of recently ground coffee.

But after numerous alarms where nothing much happened we became increasingly casual, almost fatalistic. "If that bomb has your name on it, you cannot outrun it" was the bravado statement most commonly heard in the streets. My family was comprised of people of faith, so fatalism was not part of their thinking. But the time came when we no longer dashed to the "shelter" each time the sirens blared.

Our thinking and attitudes were greatly helped by a house guest called Captain H.S. May, an officer in the Royal Artillery. One night he took me to the top story of our house and, taking out his watch, he timed the number of seconds between the flash of an explosion and the "thump" of the detonation. Then, having explained how much faster light travels than sound – alas, I have now forgotten! – he showed me how to calculate how far away the bombs were landing. Never very far, I might add. We knew that the orange glow interspersed with vivid white flashes in the sky and the endless stream of tracer shells and the sweeping arcs of the searchlights showed that "Barrow was catching it again." We knew that homes, factories, schools, and churches were burning and people were dying.

For the moment at least we knew we were safe, but we lived our lives on the shifting sands of uncertainty. We wanted it all to end. We longed for peace.

Some of our neighbors who were either too old or too infirm to be sent off to the war were recruited to serve at home. Variously described as "ARP" (Air Raid Precaution) workers or "LDV" (Local Defense Volunteers), they were equipped with a gas mask, a "tin hat" – our irreverent name for a steel helmet – and an armband identifying their status and role. And I must not forget the whistle, the closest thing to a weapon that had been given. The whistle was to be used to warn of impending danger – though we were not quite sure what to do with the danger. Most often, we used the whistle to alert people to the fact that their drapes were allowing a sliver of light to escape and possibly warn a vigilant Luftwaffe pilot of our quiet presence.

Accordingly, we either meticulously drew the drapes before switching on the lights or, if we wished to look out, we did so from a room shrouded in darkness. When we decided to watch an air raid in the dark, the room would be lit up intermittently with the brilliant light of exploding bombs. It was in these flashes of light that something incongruous about the small room from which we watched the bombing could be seen.

On the wall right next to the window was a small plaque. It was simple, oval-shaped with a flowery border in which a couple of bluebirds perched and it bore the words:

Thou wilt keep him in perfect peace,
whose mind is stayed on Thee.
Isaiah 26:3

I cannot in all honesty say that as a young boy – I was fourteen when the war in Europe finally ended with Germany's surrender – I spent any time pondering the apparent incongruity of a Bible verse that promised "perfect peace" and the reality that I was spending my adolescence in a war zone. Small boys rarely wax philosophical. All I knew was that I wanted the war to be over and for peace to be restored. I knew that was what my parents wanted, and everybody was saying there would be better days for all of us when the war was over. That was the main topic of conversation as it became increasingly apparent that the Allies were winning.

I suppose if I had given any careful thought to the biblical text, I would have equated "perfect peace" with the end of hostilities. And I suspect that was the general attitude of the people in our little town. Rationing would end and we could eat bananas again! (I had seen pictures of bananas but I had no recollection of ever having eaten one.) The men would return from the Japanese prisoner-of-war camps, and they would be just fine. No more "black-outs" – the name for the screening of windows lest we incur the wrath of a whistle-blowing ARP man.

And even though many of the locals paid no attention when, in the pre-war days, the church bells rang on a Sunday morning to call them to prayer, the thought of the church bells ringing again without heralding an invasion of jackbooted enemy troops goose-stepping through Market Square was exciting and reassuring. Loved ones would be reunited, and they would be free to set about living happily ever after.

All would be well. As the popular song broadcast repeatedly assured us:

> *There'll be bluebirds over*
> *The white cliffs of Dover,*
> *Tomorrow, just you wait and see.*

I had never seen a bluebird, or the white cliffs of Dover. But no problem!   All would be right with the world.

And that would be peace.

Perfect!

chapter 2

You Have Got to Be Kidding

In early 1945, the war in Europe ended. I remember waking up one night to the joyful sounds of the pealing bells of St. George's Church. I jumped out of bed, ran to the window, and (after checking the lights were out) I drew back the drapes. I need not have worried. Every house on St. George's Road, the street where I lived, was ablaze with light. Every light in every room of every house seemed to be shining defiantly into the night air. The usually dark row of houses looked like an ocean liner leaving port on a festival cruise. And the stolid British people who for years had learned to "grin and bear it" were letting down their hair and kicking up their heels at the same time. They were dancing in the streets. I called out to my dad, "What is going on?" I will never forget his reply. "The war is over. Peace has broken out everywhere!"

Years earlier I had listened uncomprehendingly as the authorities announced "the outbreak of war." My dad was reversing the idea. *There had been an outbreak of peace!*

The euphoria lasted for a while, but then things returned to normal. Bananas did not suddenly sprout from shelves. Food did not pour into the UK, as had been expected. Rationing continued. Some men returned to their families from the "front" forced to deal with unfaithfulness. Marriages collapsed under the strain. Jobs were hard to find. Political tensions came to a boil and the great war hero, Churchill, was unceremoniously removed from office. He was accused of being a "warmonger," and the people who had gone through enough war to last them a lifetime were in no mood to trust him to "manage the peace."

Still more ominously, talk of an "Iron Curtain" began to circulate. In a famous speech given at Westminster College, Fulton, Missouri, on March 5, 1946 – less than six months after WWII officially ended – Churchill declared: "An iron curtain has descended across the continent." He was referring, of course, to the emerging threatening power of Communism, of Marxist/Leninism, as practiced and promulgated by the Soviet Union.

And Churchill was not alone. Dr. Goebbels, Hitler's infamous information minister, had said the same thing in February of 1945 when he warned quite accurately of the dire consequences of Soviet control in Eastern Europe. President Truman was made aware of Churchill's premonitions in June of 1945. And before we had time to enjoy the fact that Hitler and his threats were gone, we were introduced to the menacing vision of our former hero, Stalin, the conqueror of the German army on the eastern front, as our archenemy.

In other words, while the celebrations of peace were taking place, the people who really knew what was going on were well aware that it was a paper-thin peace. It was certainly not a perfect peace. They knew that while the great and terrible Second World War had ended and peace had been declared and celebrated, this did not mean that hostilities had ceased. New conflicts were being born; and subsequent events showed how right they were to be concerned.

While it is true that for more than 60 years we have been mercifully saved from a third European conflict that involved the whole world ("WWIII"), this, of course, does not mean that war has ended and perfect peace has reigned. A quick glance at a timeline of military history on the web will show graphically that since the end of WWII, not a single day has gone by without a war being waged somewhere on this planet. *Not one day.* In fact, numerous wars have raged every single day!

And today we find ourselves embroiled in a new kind of war. It is called terrorism. It is a war that seems to engulf our world as it keeps people on edge, wondering where the next attack may take place. And the thought of nuclear weapons falling into the hands of those who hate Western civilization strikes fear into many hearts.

Our fond hopes of peace as *the cessation of hostilities* were not realized. They never have been realized. But the verse on my bedroom wall still insisted:

> *Thou wilt keep him in perfect peace,*
> *whose mind is stayed on Thee.*

As time went on, I became aware of the candid words of Jesus to His disciples: "You will hear of wars and rumors of wars ... such things must happen ... nation will rise against nation, and kingdom against kingdom."

"Such things MUST happen," He said. Jesus recognized a certain inevitability about ongoing conflict in our world. These are chilling words. Sobering thoughts.

Now it is not only war that robs us of peace. There are innumerable causes of conflict and tension. There is no shortage of events and people and situations and possibilities that cause worry, induce anxiety, and generate fear. But warfare portrays these various causes in their most alarming colors and certainly provides a powerful metaphor descriptive of the issues we face in the lives we lead.

So we "battle cancer," we "fight for our rights," we "wage war on poverty," we "mobilize our forces" against various ills, and we "refuse to surrender" until we have achieved our objectives. Some of our best ideas "bomb" and our greatest aspirations "get shot down" while others are "torpedoed" and "sink without a trace." Our choice of language suggests that consciously or subconsciously we think of "life as war" and, accordingly, we call our intense desire for solutions to life's trauma "a search for peace."

So the peace we seek becomes more than that which comes from the *cessation of hostilities*. It is also related to the *eradication of stress*.

Peace to a young mother frazzled with the constant demands of caring for three small children is a weekend when the kids go to grandma's place. To the veteran sailor peace is sailing into the home port on the battle-scarred cruiser and seeing his wife on the jetty holding the one-year-old son he has never held in his arms. And for the 55-year-old, retired, self-made billionaire, peace is a luxury yacht sailing the crystal clear waters of the south seas far from cell phones, microphones, as well as voice mails, snail mails, e-mails, males, and females. As for the college student, peace is when the finals are finally finished and he can just "hang" with his friends. While for the less fortunate, peace may be nothing more than the sight of blue-helmeted "peacekeepers" from the U.N. tentatively holding at bay the smoldering ethnic tensions that over the years have insisted on coming to a periodic boil.

There can be no doubt that the desire for hostilities to cease and for pressures to go away – *for peace* – is a universal longing. Our television screens are full of pictures of refugees around the world fleeing for their lives, of bereft mothers of a hundred nations mourning their sons, of mutilated young men of many an ethnic group bravely learning to walk again, of flag-draped coffins borne by grim-faced colleagues in full-dress uniform. All of these images speak loudly and clearly of the pain, sorrow, disappointment, and hollow "emptiness of soul" that people around the world wish would go away. And this speaks of the desire for something considerably better.

The sad stories on the screens are sponsored and interrupted by advertisers offering wonder-working products guaranteeing us relief from back ache, constipation, acid indigestion, anxiety fits, and other assorted ills. Attractive pitch men and women introduce us to mortgage dealers who will assuage our worries about monthly payments, refinancing schemes that will banish our indebtedness, banks that will lend us money that will buy us solutions. They must be touching a nerve somewhere and scratching where someone itches. Indeed, somebody must be watching and listening and buying their products or they would be off the air!

Human experience demonstrates that we have an innate longing for pain and pressure, all that spoils and hinders and pollutes and mars, to go away ... and for something, anything, to take its place.

We call it peace.

In the same breath that He talked about wars and the inevitability of conflict, Jesus also talked about the inevitability of "famines and earthquakes." When I read that I thought, "I have gone through my share of war but at least I have been spared famines and earthquakes." But I knew enough history to know that down through the centuries millions have experienced such horrors, and there seems to be no end to the troubling, frightening events to which people are daily exposed. But Jesus' comment on the inevitability of stress and strain was simply, *"See to it that you are not alarmed"* (Matthew 24:6)!

Was He serious?

We do get alarmed. We do fear the worst. The known possibilities are deeply disturbing. The unknown possibilities are often more disconcerting. Granted, much, if not most, of what we dread never happens. Mark Twain was speaking for many of us when he said, "My life was full of terrible problems, most of which never happened."

My wife, Jill, says that as a girl she feared her parents would die and leave her and her sister orphans. Her parents lived to be grandparents numerous times. Then as an adolescent she worried that she would never marry. When she did marry, she dreaded the thought of being childless. When our children were born, she just knew they would fall in the washer and drown. They carefully gave the washer a wide berth. When eventually they married, she worried that they would be childless. And now that we have thirteen grandchildren, she worries they may be left as orphans and so *ad infinitum*! Most of her terrible problems never happened but the thought of them took its toll.

It is not just wars and famines and earthquakes that destroy our sense of well-being. It is the thought of them. It is the possibilities. The uncertainties. The insecurities. And Jesus said, *"See to it that you are not alarmed."* That seems as unrealistic as the promise on the wall of my bedroom seen in the flash of detonating bombs!

Tell your neighbor who just lost his job and whose kid has just been arrested for dealing crack, "Do not be alarmed." He might punch you! Quote "Thou wilt keep him in perfect peace" to a businessman being audited by the IRS and he may not become violent, but he might say something quite uncomplimentary.

Do not be alarmed? Perfect peace? These folks might well say: "You have got to be kidding. There is no such thing."

But despite their skepticism they long for something of that nature. They can remember times when they enjoyed peace – if even for a brief moment. It came and they thought it would never leave. It left and they wondered if it had ever come. They grasped it, and it slipped away like mercury through their fingers; they knew it, and it drifted out of their experience like a sailboat merging invisibly into a bank of fog.

All this raises huge questions. We worry about real and imaginary problems but Jesus tells us, *"See to it that you are not alarmed."* We live with the daily trauma of life in a less than perfect world, and the Bible assures us that God will give us "perfect peace." So what are the questions raised by all this dissonance?

Is it possible to live in a stressful world and not be alarmed as we are directed? Is it realistic to live in the midst of circumstances beyond our control and experience something called "perfect peace"? Or could it be that the Bible is hopelessly out of touch with reality, that its promises are strangers to relevance, and its commands should be treated with benign neglect?

chapter 3

What Is This Thing Called Peace?

Let us consider the Bible for a few minutes. There is no doubt it has been around for a long time and that it still seems to sell well. There is also little doubt that it has been the inspiration for much that is admirable in Western civilization – the dignity of the individual, the concept of freedom, the application of justice, the sanctity of life, the institution of marriage and family.

Not only that, it has had a profound influence for good when introduced into regions of the world where it was previously unknown. Countless thousands – millions – of people living in widely diverse cultures in vastly different circumstances have derived comfort, direction, and encouragement from it down through the centuries. Philosophers wrestle with it, artists are inspired by it, politicians quote it, theologians study it, the devout devour it, unbelievers argue with it. It has been and continues to be a force to be reckoned with. Only those totally unacquainted with it would be unwise enough to suggest it is irrelevant.

Having said that, it must be admitted that the relevance of the Bible is not always readily apparent. The statement we are considering is a case in point. What is the relevance of a promise of "perfect peace" when we all know there is no such thing as a totally trouble-free environment? Why even consider the possibility of "perfect peace" when history shows that the world in which we live is constantly torn apart with wars, famines, and earthquakes? And if the New Testament records Jesus' gloomy prediction that wars and the like will continue, why would the Old Testament apparently contradict Him by holding out a tantalizing vision of perfect peace?

The two most likely answers to these questions are that the Bible is irrelevant at best, and dangerously misleading at worst. Or that the perfect peace of which it speaks and which it categorically offers is not what we assume from a casual reading. I think you will agree that it is not wise for anyone to dismiss what the Bible says without having ensured that we understand precisely what it is saying. Arriving at a conclusion without first arriving at an understanding is not the way to go. Before deciding "perfect peace" is an impossible dream we ought to make sure we know what perfect peace looks like. To do otherwise is to emulate the example of the longshoreman who was on strike. When asked why he was on strike he replied forcefully, "I do not know, but I am not going back to work until I get it!"

The biblical writer in question was the Prophet Isaiah of Jerusalem. He lived more than 700 years before Christ. He obviously came from a family of some standing, which meant that he had access to the corridors of power in Jerusalem and so was well informed about the events of his day.

In his early years Judah was prosperous under the godly rule of King Uzziah, but after he passed away less enlightened leadership took over and the ominous power of the Assyrians – a cruel and warlike people – came into ascendancy. These were precarious times. Neighboring Israel fell to the Assyrians after a merciless time of siege, and eventually Jerusalem, the capital city of Judah, was threatened with invasion from three sides. It was rather like modern-day Israel, when she was attacked simultaneously by Syria, Jordan, and Egypt. Having seen what happened to Israel and knowing the relentless power of the adversaries at their gates, the people of Isaiah's day were (not surprisingly) stricken with fear.

Under these circumstances the people of Judah were presented with two options. They could believe the messages God had sent to them through prophets, like Isaiah, that He had Jerusalem on His heart, that the king who sat on the throne was in the line of the great king David through whom God's purposes for His people would be brought to fruition, and that if He was trusted, honored, and obeyed, then He would work on their behalf. Or, alternatively, they could reject such "spiritual" concepts and look for political solutions to their dilemma. That meant entering into treaty relations with those whom God's people had no business making alliances.

As the main spokesman for the Lord had spoken long and often, Isaiah clearly and unambiguously warned that to take the latter course was a surefire route to disaster. The king took that course anyway.

So the dark clouds of warfare were looming with little hope of deliverance and bleak prospects for survival. Isaiah's predictions of Jerusalem's fate were terrifying but his warnings were ignored.

Incredibly, Isaiah decided that it was time to write a song and sing it to the people. He decided, in other words, that the best way to address the impossible situation was to communicate a message in song! But it was not a wartime masterpiece designed to quicken the blood and set the feet to marching. Neither was it a patriotic piece that would lift heads, swell chests, and "nerve the faint endeavor."

Rather, it was a song celebrating the fact that even though the people were rejecting God and would inevitably suffer the consequences when their enemies overpowered them and made their city "a heap of rubble," a day would come when the Lord would ultimately triumph and His faithful people would be like a "strong city" built on the Lord who is "the Rock eternal." It's quite a song (see Isaiah, chapter 26).

And one piece of Scripture in that song Isaiah wrote and presumably sang – perhaps you have already guessed it – was this:

> *Thou wilt keep him in perfect peace,*
> *whose mind is stayed on Thee.*

So these words were penned and performed under huge stress in the face of impending disaster. But they offered a ray of hope to Isaiah's beleaguered friends, relatives, and neighbors and spoke words of radiant possibility to the hopeless and the helpless.

But they were ignored. The people did not listen.

So now we can see the circumstances under which the promise of "perfect peace" was given, and also the cynical reaction of the people to what seemed a preposterous and unacceptable spiritual answer to an intensely practical political problem.

I wonder if my mother understood the appropriateness of the words on the simple plaque that she hung in my bedroom before the war had started. I do not know the answer to that, but when she hung that plaque, we in England awaited an invasion just as did the Jerusalemites. And while Millom in the 1940's was markedly different from Jerusalem 2,600 years earlier, the citizens of both, I have no doubt, knew fear and longed for peace.

But was the message of Isaiah as relevant to a boy living in twentieth century England as it was to a king trembling in his palace in eighth century Jerusalem?

What precisely was the message in its original form?

What was the peace of which he spoke? Clearly it was something that Isaiah believed the people could experience in some measure under pressure. It was more than a hope against hope that the fighting would stop, because Isaiah knew that the war would continue because the people had rejected the advice he had given them from the Lord.

So the peace he offered did not depend on the cessation of hostilities or the eradication of stress ... *it went much deeper.*

chapter 4

Perfect Peace

The Hebrew word that Isaiah used and which is translated "peace" in our English Bibles is *shalom*. It occurs more than 250 times in the Old Testament. In modern Israel it is still used as a greeting.

So if you visit Jerusalem today and walk through the bustling narrow streets of the Old City, you will undoubtedly be greeted by an Israeli who will leap off his stool, smile broadly, gesture expansively towards his wares stacked in colored array, and say, "Shalom!" He will urgently invite you inside to do business – on promise of a free Coke.

Now, what does his greeting convey? That he wishes

you "peace"? Yes and No.

He certainly wants you to enjoy peace although he knows as well as you do that at any moment a terrorist bomb could explode within a hundred yards of his store. And he knows exactly where his loaded automatic rifle is in case, as an army reservist, he is called at a moment's notice. He lives in violent times in a troubled part of the world, and he wishes for peace. And he wants you to experience peace, but in his mind shalom is much more than what we mean by peace. The same was true for Isaiah.

What the ancient Hebrews and the modern Israelis mean by shalom is not easily explained because it has many facets, like a fine diamond. I checked out a number of definitions of *shalom*, which illustrates the point.

- "Shalom however is perhaps better translated into contemporary English as 'flourishing' than as 'peace.'" [1]

- "Shalom goes beyond the absence of hostility to fulfilment and enjoyment." [2]

- "Shalom is the opposite not so much of war as of any disturbance in the communal well-being of the nation." [3]

- "Shalom is often indicative in the Old Testament usage of a comprehensive kind of fulfillment or completion indeed of a perfection in life and spirit which quite transcends any success which man alone even under the best of circumstances is able to attain."[4]

- "Shalom is ultimately the gift of Yahweh. ... Jeremiah, in particular also proclaimed that Yahweh withdraws his shalom in judgment."[5]

So *shalom* "is the opposite not so much of war." This is very good news, because if it is connected to the absence of war, you and I will never experience it, given that wars and rumors of wars will continue. Obviously, a person's feelings of well-being are more likely to be healthy after, rather than during, warfare. *But* shalom *suggests to you and me that it can be experienced in real measure even while the conflict continues.* It "goes beyond the absence of hostility to fulfillment and enjoyment."

If that is true, then it follows that our search for peace should not be primarily invested so much in attempts to get hostilities to cease, laudable and necessary as such endeavors undoubtedly are. Nor should it be primarily focused on eradicating stress, appealing as the thought undoubtedly is. Instead, we must move in some other direction for the simple reason that neither conflict nor stress will be totally eradicated.

Where then should we turn? Where then is *shalom* to be found?

The story of Gideon is one of my Old Testament favorites. It is recorded in the book of Judges, chapter 6, and it relates how Gideon was "threshing wheat in a wine press." This statement is made in a very matter-of-fact manner, but, in actuality, Gideon's behavior was most peculiar.

Normal people threshed wheat by taking it to a flat piece of rock in an open space, beating on the wheat and then throwing it in the air so that the wind could separate husk from grain. On the other hand, wine presses were small, confined, rock-hewn tubs in which the grapes were placed and compressed as maidens danced gaily upon them to squeeze out the juice. So a wine press was the last place you would thresh wheat, for obvious reasons.

Nevertheless, Gideon was doing just that and for good reasons. His nasty neighbors, the Midianites, constantly made life miserable for Gideon. They regularly cast covetous eyes on his harvest, watching carefully as it ripened, and at the critical moment of harvest would raid the fields, helping themselves to the fruits of his labor. They would carry home his harvest, and he would be left to contemplate the husks and straw. So he was trying to get a move out ahead of them.

While Gideon was engaged in this activity, the angel of the Lord came and said, "The Lord is with you, mighty warrior." Now obviously Gideon did not exactly look like a mighty warrior, and he was not too sure the Lord was with him, either. So he retorted, "If the Lord is with us, why has all this happened to us?"

Sound familiar? Anyway, to cut a long story short, the angel convinced Gideon not only that the Lord was with him but that he should be glad about it, because the Lord had something in mind. He gave instructions that Gideon should take his father's prized bull and kill it, tear down his dad's altar, cut down his Asherah pole (which he should never have built in the first place), and generally stir up trouble – and then declare war on the Midianites!

Having communicated all this scary news, the angel of the Lord then said to Gideon: "Shalom!" Can you believe that? He is being told to get his father madder than a wet hornet, he is going to disrupt the whole family, he is going to get everyone into a war, and the Lord talks about "Shalom-Peace!" Knowing all this, Gideon built an altar and you'll never guess what he called it: "Jehovah Shalom – the Lord is Peace!"

Pop that one in the back of your mind while I tell you another Old Testament story. This one is about King David who appears in his advancing years to have lost his direction and his senses. This story can be found in 2 Samuel, chapter 11.

Instead of going off to war at the time of year when annual scores were settled, David sent his men and stayed home himself. He hung around the palace and got involved with the young wife of one of his soldiers. The girl got pregnant, and David (knowing full well that everyone could count nine months and reckon that her husband was away when she conceived) decided he had better bring her husband home for some well-advertised "R & R."

Seeing he was commander in chief, King David had no problem ordering the young soldier home, and on arrival, he interviewed him on the conduct of the hostilities. So he asked about the soldiers, the general, and how the war was going. Not that he cared, of course! But the interesting thing about this story is what he actually said. Literally, he inquired about the *shalom* of the soldiers, the *shalom* of the general, and the *shalom* of the war! That is right – he actually inquired about the *shalom* of the war.

Now if *shalom* means absence or cessation of hostilities, then he was talking nonsense. It would mean he was asking about the end of hostilities for the men whose job it was to initiate them, the end of hostilities of the man in charge of hostilities, and the end of hostilities of the hostilities! You have the same problem with the Gideon story. Gideon was building an altar to the God who ends hostilities, at the precise moment he ordered Gideon to start hostilities.

But when David talked about *shalom* he was actually asking, "Are things going well? Are things in order? Is everything under control?" And in the same way Gideon was saying, "Things are in order because Jehovah is in charge."

And there you have the clue to what *shalom* really means. *Shalom* is all about the sense of well-being – irrespective of circumstances – that comes from knowing the Lord is in charge, and all is well.

Now if we can go back to Isaiah for a moment, we can see why he was singing. Even though from a human perspective things could not have been much worse, he was convinced that God knew what He was doing and would do it. And this gave him something to sing about! He was not ignoring his circumstances, neither was he discounting the problems they all faced. *He was putting them in perspective.* And the same was the case with Gideon.

Isaiah said another thing that is relevant to what we are considering:

This is what the LORD says –

your Redeemer, the Holy One of Israel,

"I am the Lord your God,

who teaches what is best for you,

who directs you in the way you should go.

If only you had paid attention to my commands,

your peace would have been like a river,

your righteousness like the waves of the sea."

(Isaiah 48:17-18)

Once again we have a promise of peace – in this case, it is peace like a river. This peace is promised to those who recognize the Lord, acknowledge that He knows what is best, tells us what it is, directs us in the correct manner to behave, communicates His desires through commands (not suggestions), and promises that if we do what He says, then the result will be *peace like a river!*

In other words, if we *order* our lives according to the *orders* of an *orderly* God, the result will be a sense of order. Shalom. Peace. Externally, there may be – as there was in Isaiah's case – chaos, dread, and danger, but internally, we may enjoy the peace that comes from knowing that God is in charge.

Augustine, the Bishop of Hippo in North Africa, caught the idea beautifully when he defined peace as *"the tranquility of order."* I like that. It gathers together all those words used by the theologians to define *shalom*.

That being the case, our search for peace may need to be redirected. The objective will no longer be primarily to resolve every conflict and negate every stress factor. That does not work anyway. Rather, the focus will be on carefully and diligently ordering our lives according to God's orders.

It is worth noting that Isaiah went on to say not only that our peace would be like a river, but also that our righteousness would be like the waves of the sea. In other words, when the orderly life is established, the result is a life of righteousness – living rightly before God among people – that will be as consistent as the relentless breaking of the waves against the cliffs.

We should not fail to note, either, that the chapter ends with the serious reminder:

"There is no peace," says the LORD, "for the wicked."

The wicked in this case are those ordinary folks like you and me who decide we do not want the Lord to teach us what is right. We do not wish to go in the way that we ought, we do not like taking directions from God (or anyone else for that matter), and we have not paid attention to what He commanded. The result has been we have lived lives characterized by something far removed from orderly living, according to His standards. As Isaiah put it, that is living with "no peace."

One more thing before we move on. You remember that the verse on my bedroom plaque talked about "perfect peace." You may have noticed that I have not dwelt on the adjective "perfect." But I will now.

The reason I did not dwell on it was simply because

Isaiah did not say "perfect peace." He actually said, "Shalom, shalom – peace, peace!" That was not a scribal typo; it was an intentional statement. It means something like "the peace that really is peace," or "peace upon peace" – the real thing! Not a truce or a paper peace but a deep, lasting inner sense of well-being that will not break down, will not be abrogated, and will never be withdrawn. I guess "perfect peace" gets pretty close.

So where is this peace to be found? It is to be found in "a mind that is stayed on Thee." A mindset that decides that as God is God and knows what is best, it will settle for learning and doing what He says, trusting and anticipating what He promises, accepting and enjoying what He offers, and resting on the assurance that He will come through.

Therefore, all is well. *Peace, peace!*

chapter 5

A Different Kind of Peace

I would not be surprised if you are thinking at this point, "This is so theoretical. It is highly impractical. Give me a break. Life does not work like this at all." I can understand that reaction. But let me tell you a story.

You may not have heard of Horatio Gates Spafford. He was a Chicago businessman who invested heavily in real estate in downtown Chicago and lost most of it during the devastating fire of 1871. Round about the same time, his only son died. But despite his losses, Spafford devoted considerable time and resources to assisting the thousands of people left homeless and destitute by that horrific fire. Sometime later he and his wife decided that the family needed a vacation and plans were made for them all to travel to Europe. But at the last moment, Spafford was delayed. So his wife and four daughters sailed together on the *Ville de Havre.*

Off the coast of Newfoundland their ship collided with the "Loch Earn" and sank in twenty minutes. Mr. Spafford, back home in Chicago, heard of the tragedy and awaited news of his family. It came in the form of a two-word telegram from his wife: "SAVED ALONE." His four daughters had drowned in the icy Newfoundland waters; his wife had clung to wreckage and been rescued. As soon as possible he joined his wife in Europe, and together they met with their friend, Dwight L. Moody, the evangelist, who deeply commiserated with them on their desperate loss. But Mr. Spafford replied quietly, "It is well. The will of God be done." *Incredible!*

Still later – we are not quite sure when – Spafford wrote what has become one of our best known hymns, including the remarkable stanza:

When peace like a river
Attendeth my way
When sorrows like sea billows roll;
Whatever my lot,

Thou hast taught me to say,
It is well, it is well
With my soul.

Notice, first of all, how he borrowed Isaiah's simile and spoke of "peace like a river." Now take a minute to think inside Mr. Spafford's head. He believed in a God who is in control of this world. Having arrived at that belief, he had logically concluded that if God was in control, then He should be in control of Spafford's life, too. That meant, among other things, that he should order his life according to the orders of this orderly God on the understanding that God would then work out His purposes in Spafford's life. Because he lived in a harsh world and was not and could not be exempt from its tragedies and traumas, the circumstances of his life could naturally be hard – unbearably hard. But he could, nevertheless, rest in the fact that God was in control and that knowledge would bring a sense of order to the chaos, and a deep sense of tranquility in the upheaval.

The tranquility of order. Peace like a river!

I have no doubt that he would have spent every remaining penny of his fortune if it would have brought back any of his children. I am sure he would gladly have taken their place on the stricken ship if it would have saved their young lives. I cannot begin to imagine the emptiness that his father's heart suffered after losing not only four daughters but also his only son. All of this on top of his devastating business losses. He knew pain, he knew anguish, he felt it all, experienced it all, suffered from it all. Just as any other human being would feel, experience, and suffer. He was not unfeeling and he was not a superman. He was an ordinary man whose mind was set on God, whom He trusted implicitly – and it showed. So he could say, "It is well. It is well."

In recent history we have had a rash of peaceful and not so peaceful demonstrations and revolutions. I think back to the Orange Revolution in Ukraine. Hundreds of thousands filled the streets of Kiev to protest the rigged elections which returned an old Communist to power. People power won – he is gone and a new government is in place.

They had a Rose Revolution in Georgia (not the one where Jimmy Carter lives, but the one where Josef Stalin was born). The same thing happened there. Crowds took to the streets, chanting and waving flags and demanding change. *They got it.*

Later it was the turn of the Syrian regime, firmly established in Lebanon. The people of Beirut took to the streets, waved their red and white flags with the cedar tree proudly featured, and refused to go home until the Syrians did. Then the focus switched to Bishtek in Kyrgyzstan, and similar things happened there. And on it goes. By the time you read this, the scenes will have changed, but not the presence of *disorder.*

When a crowd becomes energized and mobilized, the result can be an enormous power for good or ill. Each of the demonstrations in Kiev, Tbilisi, Beirut, and Bishtek could have moved into chaos in a hurry. The government could have called in the army, and blood would have been shed. Mercifully, violence was averted by and large but that is not always so.

Thinking of these scenes where crowds made such an impact, I was reminded of a similar scene enacted long before it could be recorded for posterity on film or disc and projected for all to see on screens around the world. It happened in the ancient city of Jerusalem a couple of millennia ago. It was a massive crowd demonstration that could easily have spun out of control, but did not.

That scene is what we Christians celebrate annually as "Palm Sunday." The original event took place when Jesus of Nazareth who had been making a name for Himself (positively with the common people, and negatively with the ruling elite), finally arrived as expected in Jerusalem.

You can read about it in all four Gospels. A large band of followers joined Him as He made His way to the Holy City. As word of His arrival reached those gathered there, they took off to meet Him and He found Himself in the convergence of two mighty streams of people who gathered round Him as He sat on a donkey's colt.

He had been very specific about riding into Jerusalem on this humble steed. In fact, He had given strict instructions to a couple of His disciples where to find it and how to commandeer it. The Gospel writers tell us He was so intentional about it because it fulfilled an ancient prophecy in Zechariah (9:9), which said:

> *Rejoice greatly, O Daughter of Zion!*
> *Shout, Daughter of Jerusalem!*

See, your king comes to you,

righteous and having salvation,

gentle and riding on a donkey,

on a colt, the foal of a donkey.

Over a period of three years, the people had been increasingly insistent that He should be their king. They had one, of sorts, but they gladly would have gotten rid of him if only Jesus would respond. But He had consistently demurred. He had answered their questions about His role with enigmatic statements that left them confused and frustrated.

But now He was making a statement. Zechariah said their king would come *"gentle and riding on a donkey, on a colt, the foal of a donkey."* Jesus was doing just that and obviously knew what He was doing. He was making a statement. They knew it. They knew He knew it. Their king had arrived and was ready to take His rightful place. Ecstasy!

So what did they do? They could not rush home and bring out their national flag. They did not have one. So they did what they used to do in those days – they tore down palm trees. Better than any flag, they waved enormous and green palm tree fronds furiously in the air, and then lay them in the colt's path. It was a wild and exciting scene.

The disciples had taken off their cloaks and laid them on the ground in the path of the young colt that had never been ridden. It must have taken calm hands to control such an unbroken young beast in the midst of such confusion and noise.

Presumably the disciples knew the story of Elisha, the prophet, who one day told a young assistant to go find Jehu, take him aside, anoint him as king, and then run for his life! You can read this in 2 Kings, chapter 9. So he did. Jehu's fellow officers, on seeing the young man breaking Olympic records as he disappeared in a cloud of dust, asked him, "What did that crazy guy want?" Jehu replied, "Oh, you know the sort of things he says. He is crazy."

"Yes," they replied. "But what did he tell you?"

"He told me that the Lord had told him to anoint me as king. So he did."

And the fellow officers immediately *took their cloaks*

and spread them under him on the bare steps. Then they blew the trumpet and shouted, 'Jehu is king.'"

Do you see what the disciples of Jesus were doing? They were saying, "Jesus is claiming to be king and we affirm Him and accept Him. He is king!" And the crowds went wild.

They started chanting, "Hosannah, hosannah." This is the word that was used by people asking royalty for a special favor; a request that the ones in power would hear the word and act for the benefit of the powerless. "Help! Save us!" But as the petitioners received what they asked for, the cry became something like "Saved! Helped!" It was a celebration and an acclamation.

Jesus was being hailed as the conquering hero. The crowds were generating a mass movement based on their belief that Jesus was the one who could bring them what they most wanted.

Understandably, the authorities became more nervous as the crowds swelled and the cheering and palm waving became more delirious. One of them pushed his way to Jesus and told Him to pacify the crowds. Jesus calmly responded that if He told the people to be quiet, the stones would take the place of the shouts of acclamation!

Any misgivings that the disciples close to Jesus may have brought to Jerusalem – they knew of the opposition of the elites – must surely have evaporated in the excitement of the hour.

But then they noticed something very odd. It was the response of Jesus to the crowds. Normally in such cases the popular leader, the one being affirmed and feted, raises his arms high, smiles broadly, and addresses the crowds who cheer his every word. But Jesus began to weep. More than that, He started to sob inconsolably.

Looking at the ancient city spread out before Him, He said:

If you, even you, had only known on this day what would bring you peace – but now it is hidden from your eyes.

(Luke 19:42)

"If you, even you" refers to Jerusalem, which many scholars believe means "City of Peace." So Jesus was probably saying, "Oh, Jerusalem, City of Peace, you of all people should have known what would bring you peace." But they had missed the point. Particularly "on this day,"

He stressed, the day when the King arrived, they should have understood the real meaning of peace. But they did not. And it broke His heart.

Where, then, was the disconnect between what Jesus was offering and what the people were expecting? They were thinking politically, nationally, even militarily. Charismatic leaders had come before Jesus. They had been received enthusiastically and had made ill-fated attempts to bring peace to the troubled city and its environs. But that meant a popular uprising against the occupying forces of the Romans. And so far all attempts to dislodge the awesome power of Rome had met with fierce resistance and reprisals, and the courageous leaders of the revolt had finished up rotting on a cross of wood for all to see, so that others might learn from their ill-advised attempts to bring peace to the land.

This kind of peace was what the crowd wanted. They were thinking secularly. Jesus was thinking spiritually.

The young man riding on the colt did not look like a military leader, and He certainly did not demonstrate a belligerent attitude, although He had not hesitated to physically throw out the crooked money changers in the

Temple. Zechariah, in his prescient statement made so long ago, had described the coming king as "gentle and riding on a donkey." The imagery was hardly military and certainly would not make the Roman legions shake in their metal-studded sandals. No, the peace He had in mind was something else entirely.

It is worth remembering the reaction of the disciples when Jesus told them of His plans to return to the Father. They were deeply perturbed. But He replied,

> *Do not let your hearts be troubled. Trust in God,*
> *trust also in me.*
> (John 14:1)

Then later on in the same talk He added,

> *Peace I leave with you; my peace I give you.*
> *I do not give to you as the world gives.*
> (John 14:27)

The peace they were missing was not something to be won; it was something on offer – a gift. It came not from fighting but from trusting and obeying. It was unlike anything they had experienced before. It was what Jesus called "my peace." And it would never be procured by secular means – it was totally unlike anything that "the world gives."

The people of Jerusalem were celebrating but their joy would be short-lived. In fact, Jesus went on to predict terrible events that would overtake the city in a few decades, resulting in its destruction. Like so many human longings, the peace they wanted would never materialize. And the tragedy was that a peace far better than anything they had envisioned was there for the taking. But they could not – or would not – see it.

I fear the same is often true today.

chapter 6

Peace with God

Christmas in tropical and equatorial regions is far different from the traditional Christmas of colder climates. Sure you will see images of Santa Claus dressed in his usual red fur-lined track suit. But he looks decidedly overdressed on a sun-baked beach. And the celebrators will be eating traditional food, but out of picnic hampers. There will be no skiing, skating, and sleigh rides – just swimming, sunning, and snorkeling.

December the 26th of 2004 dawned bright and balmy in the Asian tropics. But many of the tourists who had celebrated the previous night with gastronomic excess missed the dawn, rose late, breakfasted lightly, and then wandered down to the beach. There they lolled under the brightly colored umbrellas and gazed idly through their designer shades at the calm, warm clear water. The more active youngsters were parasailing and windsurfing. Gentle breezes and cool drinks. Perfect. Peaceful. Paradise.

But the calm, clear warm water held a terrifying secret. Down in the hidden depths where strange aquatic creatures never seen by human eyes were lurking, where dark cold currents were swirling, there were ominous rumblings and uneasy movements that human beings had never observed. On land the animals sensed something was wrong – and fled to higher ground. *For the ocean floor was moving.*

Huge tectonic plates, which for centuries had abutted each other, were finally giving way to irresistible subterranean pressures. With one giant, awful convulsion they collided, heaved, and piled on top of each other, and the ocean heaved with them. Portions of the ocean floor the size of cities, with ocean piled upon them for miles above, thrust the waters from them. Mountainous waves were formed and with electrifying speed they headed for the beaches where peace reigned.

But nobody knew what was coming.

Had someone gifted with supernatural prescience rushed along the tranquil beaches at that moment crying, "Run for the heights! Flee from the danger! Death is approaching with the speed and power of a thousand freight trains!", they would have been ignored, at best, and perhaps forcibly silenced, at worst. Tuxedo-clad waiters would have quickly removed the oddball and peace would have been promptly restored, while the ocean heaved, the waters boiled, and disaster headed relentlessly for paradise. Meanwhile, hotel managers would have assured the disturbed holiday-makers that there would be no more problems. And everybody would have relaxed all over again. With drinks replenished, peace would have been restored.

The prophets of Israel were the oddballs of their generation. They often tended to dress in outlandish fashion, they eschewed the normal religious rites and rituals, and they did not hesitate to use startling (even shocking) ways of getting the attention of the jaded, cynical, sometimes hostile public. And they tried over and over again to get the people to wake up to certain realities.

But the people did not want to listen. They preferred to give their attention to other self-appointed prophets who cried, "Peace, peace." Even while, as the prophets of Israel insisted, there was no peace.

As the frightening events of Christmas 2004 in the Asian tropics have shown, there is a kind of peace that can be enjoyed that hides the opposite of peace that ominously lurks hidden from the eyes of the unsuspecting. And our modern cultures have countless prophets who proclaim, "Peace, peace . . . where there is no peace."

This does not mean that places do not exist where people of means can surround themselves with luxury, hide themselves from discomfort, and purchase for themselves ease and enjoyment that might feel for a time like peace and contentment. These cloistered rich obviously do exist, and there are huge numbers of the more fortunate who enjoy luxury and live in situations that are the envy of the huddled masses of the less fortunate. And these less fortunate people, as they look longingly at the circumstances of the more fortunate, assume that if they could rise to that standard of living, then their troubles would be over and peace would reign for them as well.

But the prophetic criticism of those who assume they have life by the throat and have tamed its malevolent excesses and bought for themselves peace, is that these people – fortunate though they might be – are wrong about their understanding of peace. They need to know that the peace of which they speak and they enjoy is not the real peace. The prophets were saying that there is more to peace than social privilege, relational harmony, and easy living.

Of course, modern people do not spend much time worrying about Old Testament prophets and they spend even less time studying what the prophets wrote and said. Most of our contemporaries would be hard-pressed to name more than a couple of these intrepid old preachers.

They might show a little more interest in Jesus Christ. He was slightly more modern and not quite such an oddball as the prophets. But we need to remember that He said something quite similar. Granted He did not criticize those who say, "Peace, peace where there is no peace," in so many words. But when His disciples were troubled at His announcement that He proposed to leave them and return to the Father, He did say to them,

Peace I leave with you; my peace I give you.

I do not give to you as the world gives.

(John 14:27)

Notice carefully that Jesus specifically and intentionally differentiated between the peace that the world gives and that which He gives. You could say that the old prophets were trying to waken the people to the need for the kind of peace that Jesus later offered. And they were offering it in place of the peace the false prophets were offering, which was the equivalent to what Jesus said the world gave.

There is no doubt that the world can give you a certain kind of peace.

If you are depressed, it can give you Prozac.

If you are overworked, it can give you a sabbatical.

If you are distraught, it can give you sleeping pills.

If you are confused, it can give you counseling.

If you cannot get along with your boss, it can give you a transfer.

If you are bored, it can give you entertainment.

If you are single and lonely, it can give you a singles bar.

If you are stressed out, it can give you a lake cottage.

Great and wonderful as many of these things are (some are less than great and certainly not wonderful), they only produce the best the world can offer. Jesus and the prophets insisted we need a whole lot more.

What exactly was the peace that both prophets and Jesus insisted was the real peace? In a word, it was "Peace with God."

Let me explain.

We left the tourists relaxing on the tropical beaches of Asia totally unaware of the tsumani bearing down on them. They were enjoying peace. They were fortunate enough to be spending Christmas on one of the most beautiful beaches on earth. But little did they know that in a matter of minutes they would be swept up by a wave of unthinkable proportions and force, hurled high on the beach and into the crumbling structures of their palatial hotels and resorts, and then sucked with terrifying, irresistible power into the dark depths of the ocean. Many of them never to be seen again.

For a few short weeks the world was shocked, overawed, traumatized, and solemnized. Human frailty was acknowledged in the face of natural force. Human mortality was contemplated in the face of life's shocking transience and uncertainty. These were troubled and troubling days. But humans are resilient if they are anything, and they soon got back to popping Prozac and practicing politics and the peace they promise.

But I believe the remorseless waves of the tsunami demand and deserve more reflection. For example, the Apostle Paul made a fascinating statement in his letter to the Roman believers. He wrote:

We know that the whole creation has been groaning as in the pains of childbirth right up to the present time.
(Romans 8:22)

Now I am not suggesting that when he talked about creation groaning he was referring prophetically to tectonic plates grinding and heaving against each other on the ocean floor. But I do see a similarity here. I know that our physical world in its pristine beauty is built on a multitude of hidden faults: pristine beauty flourishing on hidden faults and fissures. We humans instinctively like to correct faults and mend fissures, because we know that imperfection points to something perfect and suggests the need for something better. So the whole creation – including you and me – which is less than perfect, bears silent witness (Paul said it actually groans!) to the fact that this created order is in need of redemption and renewal.

Everyone I know agrees that "things are not right." I get no argument when I point out that "things are not the way they ought to be." Everybody knows there is something wrong somewhere. They probably would not use or perhaps even understand Paul's dramatic language about "the whole creation groaning," but they would have no difficulty subscribing to the idea that upheavals do occur in the physical world and they are all too common in the international, the national, the social, the political, and the personal worlds in which they live. And they might even admit that the peace they work hard to create and love to enjoy is, well, *paper-thin*. Under the surface there are rumblings and upheavals that can burst to the surface in an instant. The whole creation, including the human dimension of it, is truly groaning.

I believe the problem can be described in terms of tectonic plates. We can call one "the will of God" and the other "the willfulness of humanity." God who created the creation – the redundancy is intended – wrote laws for its smooth operation, not unlike Henry Ford writing an owner's manual for his "Model T" Ford. As no one had ever seen a Model T Ford before Henry Ford made one, everyone was dependent upon him to know how it worked and what to do with it. And, I might add, what NOT to do with it!

In the same way, when God created the universe, including humanity, understandably no one had any previous experience of anything that existed, so they were naturally totally dependent on the creator to know what it was, how it worked, and what to do with it. And, I might add, what NOT to do with God's creation.

God's owner's manual – if you like – contained God's

will: His way of operating what He had made. It showed humanity what they were about, what they were for, what they should do and not do. And because humanity was an integral part of the rest of creation, He showed how what humanity did would have endless repercussions on the rest of the creation. The will of God was in place like a huge, monolithic, tectonic plate.

All would have been paradisiacal if humanity had been content with the will of God, but such was not the case. So they resisted His way, thought of a better way, threw out the owner's manual, and rewrote the instructions. That is how a fissure appeared, faults developed, and a second tectonic plate was made – a split from the original. A major fault line appeared right through the heart of creation. And the two plates, the will of God and the willfulness of humanity, have been grinding and heaving and rumbling and grumbling ever since.

The will of God for His creation has not changed. The willfulness of man constantly finds ways to resist and reject that will in favor of independent, self-centered living. And the result lies hidden not so far under the surface of many outwardly orderly and peaceful lives.

The incredibly popular TV show *Desperate Housewives* surely demonstrated the point. Outwardly beautiful and talented and living in spectacular circumstances, they are inwardly, on their own admission, *desperate!*

The problem of tectonic plates, as we have seen, is not simply that they tend to grumble and groan. There comes a point when they can release a tsunami. So it is with the age-long grinding of the willfulness of humanity against the will of God. It is only a matter of time until a tsunami is released.

This was why Jesus was weeping over Jerusalem. It was not only that the people did not understand the peace He was offering. They were not interested in the peace He gives because they had no conception of the tsunami heading in their direction. He immediately began to remind them of the impending consequences of their willful rejection of God and His will. He predicted physical consequences, which came to pass in the destruction of Jerusalem by the Romans in a matter of decades after He spoke. But He went further and spoke ominously of "The END" and warned people:

You also must be ready, because the Son of Man will come

at an hour when you do not expect him.

(Matthew 24:44)

"The end" of which Jesus spoke included His return in glory to establish His eternal kingdom based on a new heaven and a new earth – the perfect creation that the cracked and old, yet beautiful, creation we now inhabit groans and longs after.

But there is a dark side to this splendid picture of the future which Peter talked about on the day of Pentecost. He quoted the prophet Joel as he talked about "the great and glorious day of the Lord." But if you look carefully at what Joel actually said, you will note that Peter took some liberties with that quote. He altered "great and dreadful day of the Lord" – Joel's expression – to "great and glorious." (See Acts 2:20 and Joel 2:31.) So the question we should ask is: Will "the day of the Lord," or "the end," or whatever else we call it be "glorious" or "dreadful"?

The answer is: *It all depends on where you stand with the Lord.*

The willful rejection of the will of God by humanity has not gone unnoticed by God! And He has a definite reaction to it. As He is holy, righteous, and just, His holiness is deeply offended by humanity's sinfulness (which is another word for the willful rejection of God's will). His righteousness demands that, based on His offended reaction, He should do the right thing in response to humanity's actions; and His justice demands that He should judge humanity's actions justly and fairly. His holiness cannot look on sin; His righteousness cannot overlook sin; His justice must condemn sin. And He does. And He will.

Tsunami.

But God is not only holy, righteous, and just. He is loving, merciful, and gracious. So the very people who rightly warrant the righteous judgment of God are the objects of His love and can be the recipients of His grace and mercy. But they have to want mercy, they have to respond to love, and they have to embrace grace.

And therein lies the problem. The willfulness of humanity is so willful that it questions the love of God, scorns the mercy of God, and rejects the grace of God and chooses to go it alone. For those people the coming day of the Lord will be dreadful. But for those who yield to love, cry out for mercy, and joyfully surrender to grace – *it will be glorious.*

The former will face the wrath of God – like a tsunami. The latter will know "peace with God" and will be carried to higher ground.

chapter 7

Peacekeepers and Peacemakers

Most of my younger readers may not have heard of Marshal Tito. With a name like Tito he probably generates little interest and undoubtedly creates no sense of awe! But in his day, which is not so long passed, he was a very interesting man and those who lived under his thumb certainly did not treat him lightly. For Marshal Tito was the supreme ruler, the Communist headman, of Yugoslavia. Millions of people in the Balkans lived under his rule.

While there was much that they did not enjoy, they at least experienced a degree of domestic tranquility while his regime was in power. But then the Marshal passed

on, the Communist empire collapsed, and the Balkans erupted. The world watched in horror as long-standing scores were settled, vengeance that had been held in abeyance for decades was set loose, and a bloodbath ensued. Eventually, after much deliberation and hesitation, other nations intervened, the warring parties were separated, the map of the Balkans was re-drawn, new nations were born, and an uneasy peace dawned.

The armies moved back into their camps or returned to their homelands and another force entered the troubled region. Lightly armed, with limited rules of engagement and wearing military helmets incongruously painted powder blue – a color more suited to baby boys than grown men – the United Nations' peacekeepers arrived. Their job: *peacekeeping!*

Their presence did not mean that Serbs and Croats and Albanians and Bosnians suddenly fell in love with each other or that Muslims and Orthodox and Catholics ironed out all their long-standing differences. Far from it. The presence of the peacekeepers was more in the nature of a referee hurriedly stepping in between two American football players squaring off after an over-zealous tackle. Their role, despite their title, was not so much to keep the peace as to separate the protagonists, for the peace they were commissioned to keep had barely been made. We human beings make peacemaking so difficult that we often have to settle for peacekeeping, fully recognizing that the peace being kept hardly merits the name.

I would like to explore this idea of peacemaking in light of the conflict between the will of God and the willfulness of humanity: the two tectonic plates. If it is true that the human condition is such that we find ourselves habitually at odds with God and accordingly in danger of His tsunami-like judgment, the question we must ask is: How does one avert the judgment? How can peace with God be made?

The answer can be found in a Scripture that at first sight seems very hard to understand. In fact, some people find it downright objectionable. I refer to Paul's letter to the believers at Colossae, in which he writes:

> For God was pleased to have all his fullness dwell in
> him (Jesus Christ), and through him to reconcile to
> himself all things, whether things on earth or things
> in heaven, by making peace through his blood, shed
> on the cross.
>
> (Colossians 1:19-20)

In simple language, that means that God sent Jesus into the world fully equipped with all that it would take to fulfill the daunting task of reconciling heaven and earth. To say that heaven and earth needed reconciling is another way of saying that God and mankind were at odds, that "will" and "willfulness" were in conflict, and that God wanted things put in order. But how was this to be done? This is where the verse becomes hard for some. The answer is that God puts things to right,

by making peace through his (Jesus Christ's) blood,
shed on the cross.

That statement needs unpacking. That Jesus Christ died on the cross is largely accepted by many, if not most, people in the Western world. The remarkable popularity and impact of the film *The Passion of the Christ* speaks to the curiosity, the confusion, and the interest of huge numbers of people in the cruel death of this historic figure. But was His crucifixion just a young man dying because He was too rash in His attempts to change His culture? Was He a brave man showing us how to face adversity? Was He a remarkable man demonstrating love of the highest degree? None of these answers, while they may hold an element of truth, gets us even close to the real answer. We have to see this statement in its historic and religious context.

The Jewish people were well acquainted with a complicated intricate system of religious sacrifices, feast days, and ceremonial rites. To the casual observer they may have made little sense at all, but to the informed Jew – at least in theory – they were deeply significant. The Jews were made painfully aware by their prophets that their God was holy and that they were not. They knew that their unholiness was offensive to God's holiness and that they were in trouble before Him. But they also knew that forgiveness for their sinfulness was available. At a cost. If they were to get right with God, they had to make a sacrifice, and the sacrifice had to die. They had been told that the only way sinfulness could be dealt with was through death (it was called the shedding of blood), and so they regularly sacrificed not themselves, and not their children, but their animals.

To the Jews, this was understood. But to uninformed Western ears this sounds bizarre at best and disgusting at worst. To animal rights advocates, it is nothing short of criminal. Killing innocent animals in order to placate an offended God?

The problem, as I see it, is that we do not understand the intensity of the holiness of God and the perversity of the sinfulness of humanity – i.e., how good God is and how bad we are.

Jonathan Edwards, the brilliant Puritan preacher and philosopher from centuries ago, delivered a famous sermon entitled, "Sinners in the Hands of an Angry God." Some schools actually include the sermon in their curriculum for English classes. Sadly, this teaching often elicits embarrassed snickers from students and less than complimentary comments from teachers. In fact, the notion of God as angry – or righteously indignant – is so unacceptable to modern thinking that many people today are offended by it. Humans are offended at the very idea that God might be offended! Indeed, I have often thought that perhaps it might not be a bad idea to preach a sermon on the contemporary scene called, "God in the Hands of Angry Sinners."

If we were even to begin understanding the seriousness of sin and its repercussions in our relationship with God, we would have a better understanding of why sacrifice is necessary for forgiveness. We characterize sin now as "errors of judgment." We explain sin now as the unfortunate and inevitable result of the mistakes of others. We deal with sin now by apologizing IF anyone has been hurt by our actions. And, should we even consider sin seriously when we see it in terms of human relations rather than primarily as a divine-and-human issue? No wonder Dr. Karl Menninger, the eminent psychologist of a previous generation, asked in a book of the same name, "Whatever became of sin?"

Sin is a slap in the face for God.

Sin is a human being telling God that what He says is irrelevant.

Sin is mankind demonstrating that he has a better idea how to live than God.

Sin is a person telling the Deity that he is wiser than his God.

Sin is a human being saying to God that He does not know what is best.

Sin is a dependent human being refusing to admit his dependence.

Sin is telling God He is redundant.

Sin is man telling God His standards of what is good, right, and true are unacceptable.

God does not take this sitting down. He says, in effect: "Alright, mankind, if I am redundant, irrelevant, unnecessary; if what I say is unimportant or erroneous; if what I command is not right; and if my presence is objectionable to you – I will not impose myself upon you. You may have it your way. Operate without the embarrassment of my unwanted and unappreciated presence, input, and direction."

To many people this sounds wildly liberating. To others it sounds ominously like death.

> For if God is the source of life and I am alienated from Him, I am dead.

> For if He is the source of truth and I have rejected Him, I am living a mistake.

> For if God is the author of wisdom and I am separated from Him, I am lost in confusion.

It is death.

Spiritual death.

Alienation from God.

It is the judgment of God.

As the Apostle Paul told the Roman Christians:

The wrath of God is being revealed from heaven
against all the godlessness and wickedness of men who
suppress the truth by their wickedness, since what may be
known of God is plain to them.
(Romans 1:18-19)

This state of temporal alienation and spiritual death, if not turned around, leads to eternal separation, alienation, and death. This is the ultimate judgment: the end, the dreadful day of the Lord. The tsunami. Spiritual and eternal death are so serious that they need a radical remedy. And the only possible remedy is a substitutionary death – the death of a substitute.

And that is where the animal sacrifices came in. They were dying the death of the guilty sinners. They were accepting the consequences of a life of willful rejection. They were making a substitutionary atonement. But – and this is a huge but – it was only as the guilty confessed their sins and symbolically laid their hands on the substitutionary victim that their sin was transferred and atoned for, that their guilt was taken away.

Note that word *atonement*. It means literally AT-

ONE-MENT. Mankind estranged from God by sin and its consequences was being made AT ONE with God. But there was a problem. They had to keep repeating the procedures because the spilling of many gallons of blood could not effectively take away the continuous flow of human sin. What was needed was a monumental sacrifice that would make God and mankind "AT ONE." *Once and for all.*

But where could such a sacrificial victim be found? A sacrifice so pure, so holy, so righteous, so sinless that it would be efficacious for the sins of the whole world? And the answer was JESUS!

So when Jesus died He was

> *making peace through the blood of his cross.*

But how?

In His dying He collected the accumulated indebtedness of a sinful humanity and also collected its consequence, death. He died for all. In so dying, He presented the Father with a way to righteously judge sin and freely absolve the sinner. In dying, He absorbed the awful intensity of divine indignation, the terrible consequences of human rebellion, and the sordidness of human depravity. He satisfied the holy demands of the Father. And He left the Father free to forgive and in a position to be reconciled – to be at peace with a rebel humanity.

So, Jesus is the ultimate PEACEMAKER!

If, and this is a big if, we confess our sin and, in the same way that the guilty sinners of old laid their hands on the victim, we by faith identify Jesus as the bearer of our sin and the means of our peace with God. By *faith.*

But there is more.

In the early days when the apostles began to teach the good news about Jesus' death and resurrection, they appealed first of all to Jews and then to the rest of humanity. Traditionally there had been great divisions between the different ethnic groups. Racism is not modern, ethnic cleansing is not new, anti-Semitism was not a Nazi invention. But the early preachers insisted that if men and women from the different ethnic groups were making their peace with God, then they had an obligation to make their peace with others who had also made their peace with God. So they, like their Master, became peacemakers. In fact, Jesus said (and they took Him seriously):

> *Blessed are the peacemakers,*
> *for they will be called sons of God.*
> (Matthew 5:9)

The most amazing things began to happen. Old enemies became friends, old insults became irrelevant, old injuries were healed, old conflicts became resolved. And there was a good reason. The insults, the injuries, and the conflicts were now called by a new name: sin.

But sins had been forgiven by God and forsaken by men. So there was no need, and they had no right, to perpetuate sinful behavior in relationships and revisit sinful attitudes in feuds. New relationships could be forged, new dimensions of life discovered. Now the new believers could understand what the apostle meant when he told them:

> *Let the peace of Christ rule in your hearts,*
> *since as members of one body you were called to peace.*
> (Colossians 3:15)

A whole new army of peacemakers had been mobilized; a brand new community of peacemaking had been born. They knew that before the world could employ peacekeepers, somebody had to be a peacemaker. And they knew how to do it. For in the same way that the forgiven make great forgivers, those at peace with God understand how to bring peace on earth.

chapter 8

A Peace in Concrete

Most men know what it is to work hard in order to make their wives happy. They do not always do it but there are occasions when they finally get around to doing the chores their wives have "suggested" they should do for a couple of years. Such was the case with the man who eventually got around to digging up his driveway, and laying a fresh new concrete surface. Flushed with success and unaccustomed to the exercise required to complete the task, he surveyed it with great satisfaction. After showering and changing, he settled down in his favorite chair to read the paper, await dinner, and bask in his wife's approval.

However, his joy was rudely interrupted by the sight of the neighbor's kid walking carefully through his newly laid concrete and making footprints as he went. He rushed outside and remonstrated in violent language with the young gentleman who was undoing the work of many hours in a few short minutes. Unfortunately, the man's pastor walked past at that critical moment. Hearing his friend's threats and imprecations, he said, "I thought you loved young people!"

Mortified, the tired husband replied, "I do, pastor. But only in the abstract – not in the concrete!"

While a bit trite, it makes the point of one of life's challenges. We are called to live in the twin realms of abstract theory and concrete reality. Simultaneously. I am afraid the former often comes easier than the latter.

Some of what I have said about peace may have sounded persuasive in the abstract, although problematic in the concrete. For instance, peace with God certainly sounds a lot better than waiting for the tsunami of final judgment to overtake me. And the thought of believing all is well while all around me nothing looks that way is appealing, but sounds rather like denial. Then again, ordering my life according to the orders of an orderly God makes sense when compared with the alternative, which is to say I believe in God but deny His divine authority in my life. But still, so often I do not even bother to make the effort to do the ordering. That borders on the schizophrenic.

So how do we get from the abstract to the concrete? *How does it work?*

At some risk at this stage in this little book, let me take you back one final time to the verse on the wall of my boyhood bedroom:

Thou wilt keep him in perfect peace,
whose mind is stayed on Thee.

The peace being imparted by God, the peace that Jesus said He gives, which is unlike the peace the world gives, is not promised to everybody. It is given to the one whose "mind is stayed on Thee (God)." It starts with a mind that is "stayed." That is not a word in common use nowadays, but it means "fixed" or "focused." It is about a mindset.

I have a number of friends who are, or were, professional athletes. In everyday life they are talkative, humorous, and friendly. But on game day, they turn into something else. They put on what they call their game face. They become focused. Their minds are fixed on the task at hand. Other matters are put to one side. Objectives are clear, priorities are in place. They know what they are about. Their minds, you could say, are stayed.

Some time ago in a troubled part of the world, I asked a young couple who worked there what kind of people they needed to help them in their work. They described the people they were looking for, and when I asked how they would recognize them if they met them, they replied without hesitation – *"By the set of their jaw!"* Knowing the kind of situations in which they regularly found themselves, I knew what they meant. They needed people of conviction and commitment, people not easily diverted from their course or discouraged by their setbacks. People who know how to keep on keeping on. So they were thinking in terms of "jaw set." I'm talking about "mindset" here, and I believe these verbal expressions are first cousins.

Thinking about God in the abstract (as long as it is not wishful thinking based more on human preference than divine revelation) has a legitimate place in our lives. Learning about who He is, what He does, has done and plans to do, and what He expects of us and what He promises us, is essential. But we have to get from the abstract to the concrete. We must move from the "if" to the "then."

- *If* God is who He says He is, and can do what He says He can do, and will do what He promises, *then* ... then what? *Then* I need to ask myself if I want Him to do for me what He promises ... and at the same time I should ask myself if I want to do what He says!

- *If* God promises to give perfect peace under specific circumstances, *then* I need to believe that He will.

- *If* God says this kind of peace is available to those whose minds are "stayed," *then* I need to check whether or not I will focus on Him rather than the circumstances and allow nothing to deflect me from confidence in His ability to hold me fast and keep me strong.

Take time to read those three points again ... slowly and carefully.

There is a very helpful explanation of these steps in a letter that the Apostle Paul wrote when he was living in less than ideal circumstances in a Roman prison. He was convinced that his days were numbered – he was looking into what he believed would be a brief future that in all probability would come to a very unpleasant ending. He was right! This is what he wrote:

Do not be anxious about anything, but in everything, by prayer and petition, with thanksgiving, present your requests to God. And the peace of God, which transcends all understanding, will guard your hearts and your minds in Christ Jesus.
(Philippians 4:6-7)

He was saying similar things to those spoken by Isaiah the prophet. Basically, he was telling the people that God is not too busy to be bothered with everything that bothers us. In fact, He gives us permission to make anything that causes us anxiety a matter for prayer. We can talk to the Lord about anything and everything as long as we do so with thanksgiving. It must be with thanksgiving because that shows not only that we are thankful for the privilege of praying and for the fact that God promises to listen but more than that, thanksgiving that God will take charge.

We become anxious when we face situations that we cannot control or that we fear will get out of control. And there is no shortage of that kind of situation! But if God is God and is actively involved in the human experience, then His willingness to respond to prayers about anything and everything certainly points in this direction. He can control what we cannot.

However, we must be clear what we mean by control. If we think it means that God will take what we worry about and fix it so that everything will be hunky-dory and we will be free to relax and have a ball, then we got it wrong. Despite what some preachers on TV might tell you, God did not promise us a rose garden. Listen to what Paul wrote:

We know that in all things God works for the good
of those who love him, who have been called
according to his purpose.
(Romans 8:28)

This verse teaches us that God is actively at work in all situations, not necessarily "fixing" them but working out lasting benefits through them. The reason He does not always fix a worrisome problem is that going through the problem rather than evading or avoiding it may be in our best interests in the long run.

Many kids have found ways to miss a test only to discover they flunked a degree. It is the "long run" that matters and in God's way of looking at things it is a very long run. In fact, it stretches into eternity and this is what He does – He works through things that worry us and make us sweat down here and develops us through them so that when, in the long run, we make it to eternity we are better fitted for the experience.

Now, knowing this helps enormously. There is something very comforting and consoling in knowing that the worrisome things of life cannot be totally pointless when God gets His hands on them. And there is something really quite positive about recognizing that through the negative things you tend to worry about, God brings about positive things that you can only dream about.

So this becomes the focus.

We get up in the morning and instead of worrying about the things we cannot change – and may never happen – we put on our game face. We bring our concerns, hopes, aspirations, longings, and fears to Him in prayer, trusting He hears and cares, and believing that He will work in them all to bring about lasting fruitfulness and blessing. With this mindset we greet the day.

Now it must be admitted that something may happen during the day that makes the game face slip a little, but if we can use the athletic analogy one more time, the experienced athlete knows how to recover quickly from a mistake, put it out of his mind, and get back in the game! *So it goes for us.*

The people to whom Paul wrote about prayer, petitions, and peace lived in Philippi. It was an interesting place where many former Roman soldiers lived out their retirement. Veterans of many campaigns, they knew from personal experience what it was like to try to overcome an enemy well entrenched in a stronghold. Knowing this, Paul used a military term to describe what happens when the peace of God takes root in our lives. It will "guard" our hearts. Literally, he said our hearts would be "garrisoned." A garrison consisted of 300-1,000 soldiers.

So our hearts would be like a garrisoned town — nothing would shake the peace of mind and emotions that God gives those who learn to have a focused mind fixed on Him.

It is about mindset. Set like concrete!

One final thought. Did you notice how the peace that is offered was described? It is the peace that "transcends all understanding." Think about that for a minute, becase there is a peacefulness that is easily understood.

When I stepped down after 30 years as the senior pastor of a large church, I was surprised by the release from tension I experienced without having realized the tension was there in the first place. When I explained this unusual sensation to friends, they nodded their heads wisely. They understood. That kind of peace is perfectly understandable. The people dancing in Millom's streets were reacting to the outbreak of peace with unrestrained delight. Perfectly understandable.

But "peace peace" cannot be so easily understood because so often it defies human logic; it transcends human expectations and experience. It is a "God thing." It is His gift bought at enormous price by Jesus and presented to us by the Holy Spirit who lives in our hearts at our invitation where He busily produces His fruit – including peace. And this is a peace that goes beyond our circumstances … beyond the things that affect our lives … rooted in the very nature of God Himself.

That is *real* peace.

Shalom to you.

A Prayer

O Lord, life is full of daily temptations, constant testings, regular troubles, periodic traumas, and occasional terrors. It is tough. I struggle to cope, I battle the situations, I do my best and I long for a break – to get away, to be free for a while. Just a little peace; that is all I want. Sometimes, briefly I experience it and then like a vapor it is gone. I return to earth with a bump. But the peace You offer sounds appealing, winsome, delightful. It does not promise changed circumstances, just changed attitudes and reactions. It is all about relating to You, trusting You, honoring You, loving You, and living in the good of You and Your grace and power.

To relate to You means I have to acknowledge You as Lord of my life. This I have not always done, but I desire to make a fresh start. Relating to You is not a thing of a moment, but the practice of a lifetime. I want to develop this art. I need to refocus, I want to reorient. I deeply regret the sinfulness of my disregard of You, my disobedience to You, and my disdain for Your way of truth. I yield now to Your gracious control and look to You to pour the peace that transcends understanding into the openness of my heart and life. All this, I acknowledge gladly is possible only through the work and merits of our Lord Jesus Christ. *Amen.*

End Notes

1 New Dictionary of Christian Ethics & Pastoral Theology, ed. David J. Atkinson, David F. Field, Arthur Holmes, Oliver O'Donovan (Downers Grove: InterVarsity Press, 1995), 19.

2 Ibid., 20.

3 The New International Dictionary of New Testament Theology, ed. Colin Brown, Vol. 2, (Grand Rapids: Zondervan, 1976), 777.

4 Ibid., 778.

5 Ibid., 778.

About *Telling the Truth*

Telling the Truth, the Bible teaching ministry of Stuart, Jill, and Pete Briscoe, exists to use all forms of media to preach Christ to the nations through the clear, expositional teaching of God's Word, so that people might come to know Him – the only Way, the only Truth, and the only Life – helping each person to experience the Life of Christ in all its fullness.

Telling the Truth's daily half-hour radio program can be heard on nearly 500 radio outlets worldwide and at **tellingthetruth.org**.

Steps to Peace With God

1. God's Purpose: Peace and Life

God loves you and wants you to experience peace and life—abundant and eternal.

The Bible Says …

"We have peace with God through our Lord Jesus Christ." *Romans 5:1, ESV*

"For God so loved the world that He gave His only begotten Son, that whoever believes in Him should not perish but have everlasting life." *John 3:16, NKJV*

"I have come that they may have life, and that they may have it more abundantly." *John 10:10, NKJV*

Since God planned for us to have peace and the abundant life right now, why are most people not having this experience?

2. Our Problem: Separation From God

God created us in His own image to have an abundant life. He did not make us as robots to automatically love and obey Him, but gave us a will and a freedom of choice.

We chose to disobey God and go our own willful way. We still make this choice today. This results in separation from God.

The Bible Says …

"For all have sinned and fall short of the glory of God." *Romans 3:23, ESV*

"For the wages of sin is death, but the gift of God is eternal life in Christ Jesus our Lord." *Romans 6:23, ESV*

Our choice results in separation from God.

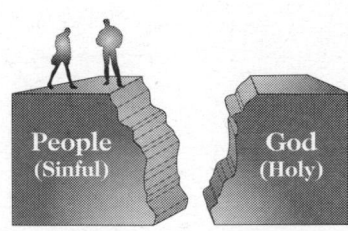

People (Sinful) God (Holy)

Our Attempts

Through the ages, individuals have tried in many ways to bridge this gap ... without success ...

The Bible Says ...

"There is a way that seems right to a man, but its end is the way to death." *Proverbs 14:12, ESV*

"But your iniquities have separated you from your God; and your sins have hidden His face from you, so that He will not hear." *Isaiah 59:2, NKJV*

There is only one remedy for this problem of separation.

3. God's Remedy: The Cross

Jesus Christ is the only answer to this problem. He died on the cross and rose from the grave, paying the penalty for our sin and bridging the gap between God and people.

The Bible Says ...

"For there is one God, and there is one mediator between God and men, the man Christ Jesus." *1 Timothy 2:5, ESV*

"For Christ also suffered once for sins, the just for the unjust, that He might bring us to God." *1 Peter 3:18, NKJV*

"But God demonstrates His own love toward us, in that while we were still sinners, Christ died for us." *Romans 5:8, NKJV*

God has provided the only way ... we must make the choice ...

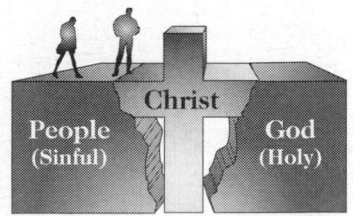

4. OUR RESPONSE: RECEIVE CHRIST

We must trust Jesus Christ and receive Him by personal invitation.

THE BIBLE SAYS ...

"Behold, I stand at the door and knock. If anyone hears My voice and opens the door, I will come in to him and dine with him, and he with Me." *Revelation 3:20, NKJV*

"But as many as received Him, to them He gave the right to become children of God, to those who believe in His name." *John 1:12, NKJV*

"If you confess with your mouth the Lord Jesus and believe in your heart that God has raised Him from the dead, you will be saved." *Romans 10:9, NKJV*

Are you here ... or here?

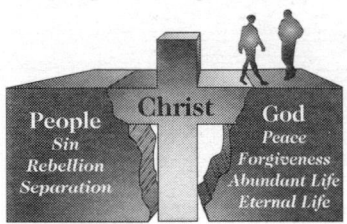

Is there any good reason why you cannot receive Jesus Christ right now?

HOW TO RECEIVE CHRIST:

1. Admit your need (say, "I am a sinner").
2. Be willing to turn from your sins (repent) and ask for God's forgiveness.
3. Believe that Jesus Christ died for you on the cross and rose from the grave.
4. Through prayer, invite Jesus Christ to come in and control your life through the Holy Spirit (receive Jesus as Lord and Savior).

WHAT TO PRAY:

Dear Lord Jesus,
    I know that I am a sinner, and I ask for Your forgiveness. I believe You died for my sins and rose from the dead. I turn from my sins and invite You to come into my heart and life. I want to trust and follow You as my Lord and Savior.

        In Your Name, amen.

_____   _____
Date   Signature

God's Assurance: His Word

If You Prayed This Prayer,

The Bible Says ...

"For, 'Everyone who calls on the name of the Lord will be saved.'"
Romans 10:13, ESV

Did you sincerely ask Jesus Christ to come into your life? Where is He right now? What has He given you?

"For by grace you have been saved through faith. And this is not your own doing; it is the gift of God, not a result of works, so that no one may boast." *Ephesians 2:8–9, ESV*

The Bible Says ...

"He who has the Son has life; he who does not have the Son of God does not have life. These things I have written to you who believe in the name of the Son of God, that you may know that you have eternal life, and that you may continue to believe in the name of the Son of God."
1 John 5:12–13, NKJV

Receiving Christ, we are born into God's family through the supernatural work of the Holy Spirit who indwells every believer. This is called regeneration or the "new birth."

This is just the beginning of a wonderful new life in Christ. To deepen this relationship you should:

1. Read your Bible every day to know Christ better.
2. Talk to God in prayer every day.
3. Tell others about Christ.
4. Worship, fellowship, and serve with other Christians in a church where Christ is preached.
5. As Christ's representative in a needy world, demonstrate your new life by your love and concern for others.

God bless you as you do.

Billy Graham

If you want further help in the decision you have made, write to:
Billy Graham Evangelistic Association
1 Billy Graham Parkway, Charlotte, NC 28201-0001

1-877-2GRAHAM (1-877-247-2426)
BillyGraham.org/Commitment

There is ENOUGH HISTORY HERE TO FILL A BARN, ENOUGH TRUTH TO FILL A HEART.

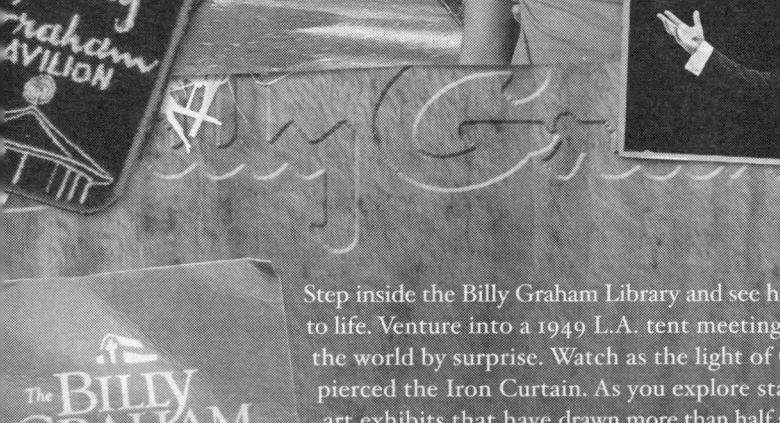

The BILLY GRAHAM Library

Step inside the Billy Graham Library and see history come to life. Venture into a 1949 L.A. tent meeting that caught the world by surprise. Watch as the light of God's love pierced the Iron Curtain. As you explore state-of-the-art exhibits that have drawn more than half a million visitors since 2007, you'll witness the extraordinary ways God used an ordinary farm boy.

Come just as you are.